God i

God in Us

A Case for Christian Humanism

Anthony Freeman

SCM PRESS

0 334 02538 9

First published 1993
by SCM Press Ltd
26–30 Tottenham Road London N1 4BZ

Fifth impression 1994

Phototypeset by Intype, London
Printed and bound in Great Britain by
Biddles Ltd, Guildford and King's Lynn

Contents

For
Jacqueline

Preface

If you
think of yourself as a Christian,
try to live a Christian life,
find solace in worship and prayer,

yet cannot believe
the supernatural teachings of the church,

this small book is offered to you
by one of like mind,
who does not aim to prove anything
or defend anything,
but rather to muse aloud for his own benefit
and that of any who may care
to eavesdrop.

I

The Way we Live Now

In lighthearted moments I have called myself and my congregation at St Mark's Church 'The Sealed Knot on Sunday'. The Sealed Knot is a band of ordinary twentieth-century folk who enjoy coming together at weekends to immerse themselves in the world of English civil war. For a few hours they adopt the dress and language and social organization of the seventeenth century and re-live, as cavaliers and roundheads, the excitements of those ancient battles of Edgehill and Naseby and Worcester. I can understand their enthusiasm. I used to be assistant curate in the parish which includes the site of the Battle of Worcester. I would stand on Redhill (named after the spilt blood) and look down to the city and the cathedral tower and imagine the young Charles II up there surveying the course of the fighting. It is not pure make-believe. It is a complex mixture of historical fantasy and a genuine desire to affirm one's roots and continuity with the past. Which brings me back to Staplefield. We gather week by week and for an hour or so on Sunday morning and we immerse ourselves in that world of the seventeenth century and – to be precise – the year 1662.

God in Us

A *changed world-view*

The Book of Common Prayer of 1662 was one of the first-fruits of Charles II's return from exile after Cromwell's commonwealth and it was already out-dated then, being almost unchanged from its first edition over a hundred years before. As we solemnly recite it today, we enter a world so different from our own, that only familiarity blinds us to the amazing change in outlook. Take for example the prayer for the Queen used at Holy Communion:

> Almighty God, whose kingdom is everlasting, and power infinite; Have mercy upon the whole Church; and so rule the heart of thy chosen Servant Elizabeth, our Queen and Governor, that she (knowing whose minister she is) may above all things seek thy honour and glory: and that we, and all her subjects (duly considering whose authority she hath) may faithfully serve, honour, and humbly obey her, in thee, and for thee, according to thy blessed Word and ordinance; through Jesus Christ our Lord, who with thee and the Holy Ghost liveth and reigneth, ever one God, world without end. Amen.

This prayer belongs to a world in which the rulers of the nations had more-or-less absolute personal power. They were subject only to God's rule and they wielded his authority. (The asides in brackets made sure that the worshippers not only prayed for their Queen but got a lesson on sovereignty into the bargain.) Now this is not the world we live in. In our own country the Queen has virtually no power today and, although a hereditary monarch, depends upon the goodwill of the people to keep her crown. In other countries, where the head of state is elected by popular ballot, this situation is even clearer. Yet we still use the prayer. Presumably it means something to us, and something to which at the end we are willing to say, 'Amen'. I can speak only for myself, but for me the prayer is an expression of hope for the well-being of our whole country which the Queen, as a figure-head, symbolizes.

It is not only the nature of earthly kingship which has changed since 1662. Our understanding of God has, if anything, undergone an even more radical change. Like his earthly counterpart, he was formerly thought of as wielding absolute power: *whose kingdom is everlasting, and power infinite.* He had direct and personal control, not only over the hearts of kings and queens, but over the whole physical universe. We no longer live in a world where such an idea has any place. If you doubt me, consider the following prayer, slightly shortened, taken from those printed after the Litany for occasional use at Morning or Evening Prayer:

For Fair Weather

O Almighty Lord God. . . We humbly beseech thee, that although we for our iniquities have worthily deserved a plague of rain and waters, yet upon our true repentance thou wilt send us such weather, as that we may receive the fruits of the earth in due season; and learn both by thy punishment to amend our lives, and for thy clemency to give thee praise and glory; through Jesus Christ our Lord. *Amen*.

I am not saying that the prayer could not be used today. What I do say is that in order to use it with any degree of integrity we should need to make the same sort of mental adjustments about God as were needed in the previous example about the Queen. The prayer could become an acknowledgment of human responsibility for upsetting the balance of the environment and a warning not to take for granted nature's ability to compensate. But it could no longer be used to mean exactly what it says. We no longer live in a world where natural disasters are understood to be God's punishment for immoral behaviour. We no longer live in a world where God is understood as having that kind of direct control over events at all.

You may want to challenge this claim. To test it, consider two assassination attempts on figures of international importance. In May 1981 the Pope was shot and almost killed. The bullet just missed hitting the spinal column and he recovered. It was suggested that divine intervention had caused a deflection and avoided fatal injury. But no one really believed that. Just think: if we really believed that God could protect his chosen ones by deflecting bullets, then one of two conclusions would have to be drawn from this case. Either God was monumentally incompetent in not upsetting the aim enough to miss the Pope altogether; or else God deliberately allowed the Pope to be injured – but not fatally. Neither suggestion was made. Because no one really believes in that kind of intervention any more. My second example is from

November 1963. President John Kennedy was shot and killed. He was the leader of the world's most powerful nation. It was a time of great international tension. If God had an interventionist day-to-day concern with world affairs it could hardly have been a matter of indifference to him. Yet no one printed headlines such as: *God's Judgment on Kennedy Administration* or *Marksman's Miraculous Aim*. The absence of any miraculous intervention to save John Kennedy went quite un-remarked. And no one suggested that his killer received divine inspiration for his excellent shooting. The thought of God's direct involvement simply did not arise, despite the great significance of the event for millions of people across the world. The reason, surely, is that no one really believes in that sort of God. Yet I have no doubt that, had the President survived as the Pope did, there would have been claims that it was a miracle.

What is really going on in cases like this? People are not stupid. They know with their brains that God does not interfere with our lives. Yet even non-religious people will say after an event, 'It was a miracle,' and religious people will even pray for one in advance. What does it all mean? It means we are using the words 'God' and 'miracle' in a new way. They are not telling us something factual and additional about the situation but they are saying a lot about our reaction to the situation. When I say of a bad accident, 'It's a miracle it was not worse,' I am expressing my relief that a potentially awful outcome has been avoided. I am not saying anything at all about the cause and course of the accident itself. And when I say, 'Thank God the Pope did not die,' I am not implying that it was God's fault that the President did die. It is a way of

5

saying that I am glad the Pope was not killed; it is not a statement about the reason why the bullet took the path it did.

I cannot tell what people in 1662 believed about God's action in the world. What I do know is that the words of the Prayer Book, if taken literally, belong to a world which is not and cannot be mine. Yet I also know that by reinterpreting the words as I go along, I am able (in many cases at least) to use the prayers. More than that, I often prefer them to many more modern alternatives. The problem is this: there comes a point where the saying-of-one-thing-and-meaning-another becomes a way of life. It can begin to spill over into other walks of life where it is less acceptable, where people expect you to say what you mean and to mean what you say. And even within the church, where everybody must be reinterpreting to some extent, ought we not to be more honest about where we stand? I made a way into the subject via the Sealed Knot and the Book of Common Prayer, but it should not be thought that the problem is caused by, or limited to, the use of seventeenth-century language. If anything the thing becomes more difficult when we use modern speech.

One of the chief failings of the Alternative Service Book 1980 is that it makes no appreciable advance theologically upon the Book of Common Prayer. It has left out one or two of the prayers which are more obviously out-dated at the human level (including the two quoted above) but it still takes for granted that world-view which has God an absolute divine king intervening in earthly affairs. That world was already becoming obsolete in 1662, with the scientific discoveries of Sir Isaac Newton and others. More recent developments in science and philosophy have removed us from it entirely. Yet it is still the world-view against which we try to frame our religious life. When we begin to say our prayers in modern rather than archaic English, this dislocation between our religious and day-to-day worlds becomes even more apparent. In such a situation, apart from burying our heads in our hands, what are we to do? There are broadly three strategies being adopted among Christians today, which for convenience (but not entirely happily) I shall label as conservative, liberal and radical (or open).

Three religious approaches

1. The conservative reaction is to remake a world in which the old landmarks are re-established. To be a member of the conservative church you have to accept this world view, which attempts to recover the old lost order of a supernatural realm and an absolutely powerful and interventionist God. In general this means sealing one's religious life from the rest of life. Like all artificially built 'worlds', this one feels threatened by the outside world. In this situation the believers will tend to live more and more of their life within the religious group, where their chosen beliefs are cherished. Such a church sees itself as continuing the traditional faith, which entails its members believing that their teaching does actually describe the universe as it really is. But that means they should be in dialogue with all other attempts – scientific, philosophical, sociological – to describe reality. The effect of their method is generally to do the opposite, to cut them off from these other disciplines by creating a self-contained and self-consistent (but for this reason ulti-

mately self-defeating) system. It is self-defeating because instead of describing the way things really are, with a relevance to us all, it has become a set of agreed 'rules of conduct and debate' for those who are 'inside the club'. Mediaeval theology was the Queen of Sciences. Modern conservative theology bears more resemblance to the Laws of Cricket. So conservative Christianity believes it is continuing a traditional faith but in fact it is creating a new faith. To believe in a supernatural all-powerful interventionist God when the rest of the world has abandoned that belief, is not the same thing as having believed in such a God when it was the generally accepted world-view. No form of Christianity in the 1990s can be the same as the Christianity of 1662, or of 1066, or of any past time, because *to say the same thing in new circumstances is to say something different*. There is no such thing – for us at least – as a timeless truth. My feeling that conservative Christians delude themselves in this matter is one of the reasons that I have never myself been tempted to take their route. At the end of the day, they seem to me like the character in 'The Goon Show': he had no watch, but could always tell you the time because he carried a piece of paper on which some kind person once wrote it down.

2. For over twenty years I followed the second strategy, that of liberal Christianity. Liberals take seriously the need to engage with the world as it is now understood. Unlike the conservatives, they accept that the expression of the truth must alter with the times. The alternative to today's outlook is not timeless truth but yesterday's outlook, and therefore we have to make do with today's. The method of liberal theology is to allow science to

explain *how* the world is, and leave theology to explain *why* it is like that. The overall effect is to keep the theory of a supernatural world, a creator, a saviour, etc. but in practice to see God as working in and through the natural order. This requires an essentially optimistic view of the way the universe is going, and that does not always tie in with experience nor with traditional Christian teaching. Liberals continue to use traditional religious language but find it embarrassing. For example, you can square the idea of a creator God with the well-regulated world of science, but how can you make sense of prayers in which you ask that same God to intervene and do things now? It can't be done, so your prayers increasingly take the form, 'Lord, help us to do things.' Somehow it is easier to imagine God's affecting my actions than to imagine his acting directly on the physical world. Or again, you can square the idea of God's inspiring the scriptures with their having a human author, but how can you decide which parts express God's absolute Word and which are merely the words of the human writer? It can't be done, so on all matters of social and ethical concern, official church reports spend many pages loyally examining the biblical evidence and then effectively ignoring it when it comes to making recommendations. It seems impossible for liberal theology to avoid looking wishy-washy and defensive. As someone has put it: if theology gets too liberal it gets boring, and if it stays exciting it stays unbelievable.

3. So what is the third strategy, which I have called radical (or open) theology? It is to admit that religion is a purely human creation. Historical enquiry over the past three hundred years has shown how the text of the Bible,

the teachings of the church, our forms of worship, etc. all have a human history. Liberals, while happy to learn more of our religious origins and development, have still held that behind the human activity lies the guiding hand of a supernatural God. Conservatives have tried to play down the human and historical element (e.g. by maintaining that the first five books of the Bible were dictated by God to Moses all at one time) and stressed the supernatural authority of their religion. Radicals say that we do not need to bring in the supernatural at all. It belongs to that long-gone world of the past. It may have a place in fairy tales and horror films but it has no place in our understanding of the real world. All aspects of our life – physical, mental, aesthetic, moral, spiritual – all are human in origin and content. To invoke the supernatural is unnecessary, because we can explain all aspects of our life without it. It is also dangerous, because it leads to our claiming supernatural and indeed divine authority for things which are in truth only human.

The claim to explain the whole of life in natural terms is not new. But in the past, when people have given up belief in a supernatural God, they have also given up their religion. Today is different because a number of people are finding meaning in a non-supernatural version of Christianity, after they have given up belief in an objective personal God. More than that, they are claiming that it is possibly the most authentic form of Christianity which can be held today. I am now among that number.

This book is my attempt to work through, for myself and with my congregation, the consequences of this shift in my own Christian belief. If it is sometimes a little contradictory, that is because I am far from having everything neatly worked out. What I do know for certain is that the old liberal dilemma – how can religion be both credible and exciting? – has been resolved. Every aspect of the faith takes on a fresh look and a new meaning. Old problems dissolve away and new challenges arise at the same moment. I am no longer trying to defend a set of received propositions which I only half accept. Instead I find myself on a voyage of discovery, creating new maps and finding my true faith for the first time.

My 'conversion experience' came at a conference last year. I suppose it was in the same general class of conversions as that of Martin Luther. Not that I would compare myself with him except in this: it was not a conversion from unbelief to faith, but from a Christianity which had become oppressive to one which brought a glorious sense of freedom and joy. This freedom came when I accepted that I did not believe in God as traditionally understood. That was a kind of trigger which released me to find a new meaning in the word God. Only when I had accepted that 'I do not believe in God' (my old God) was I free to discover how with integrity I could still say 'I believe in God' (understood in a new way).

I wonder how many other people have been converted to a new and living Christian faith by plucking up the courage to say, 'I do not believe in God'! My reason for sharing this piece of autobiography is threefold. First, to underline the importance of sharing our faith *and our doubts* and of being honest with ourselves and with others. Without the fellowship of like-minded people at the Sea of Faith conference and the support of family and friends at home I should never have been able to make the breakthrough. Secondly, to tell you how positive and enriching and liberating it has been, even though it might at first sight appear to be a negative move. And thirdly, and most importantly, to show how authentic a *Christian* experience this has been. Time and again we hear in church that we must be ready to give up even our most cherished possessions if we are to be true disciples. For years I had been clinging to my inherited belief in God: and do you blame me? To give it up would be to risk not only my religion but my reputation, my job, my home, my social world, in short my whole way of life. Yet once I did it, once I was able to admit to the possibility that I did not believe in God, wonderful things started to happen. Anxious friends asked whether I had lost my faith. I was able to assure them that I had not. I had given it away: given away my old second-hand faith and so been free to discover for the first time what I myself *really* believed. One of the things I found was that in a new way I could give real meaning to belief in God. That, surely, is authentic Christian grace. That, surely, is the *gift* of faith.

A Parable:

The Wind is Green

When John is a boy he is told that the wind is coloured green. He accepts this because he trusts the person who told him. As he gets older, John finds certain problems with this piece of information. He cannot test it as he can the colour of grass or pillar boxes. But when he asks about it, he is told that believing the wind is green is a very special piece of information precisely because it cannot be tested in the usual way. More than that, believing it should make him very happy and if he does not believe it, bad things will follow.

So John tries to make sense of this meaningless claim. He notices that the wind moves the branches of the trees more when they are in leaf than when they are bare; that the wind brings the rain which makes the grass greener in summer. The wind is certainly very strange and it does have some plausible links with greenness. Very well then, if it makes other people happy John will accept that the wind is green. But it does not make him happy. The best that he feels is relief when he finds another of those apparent connections between the wind and greenness. Most of the time it is simply a burden to be borne.

Then one day a friend says to him: you are trying to do the impossible. You are trying to believe the wind is a certain colour. But the wind is a movement of air. A movement cannot have any colour. *The category of colour is not appropriate when talking about the wind.* It is therefore *impossible* that the wind should be green or any other colour. And with that the burden is lifted from John's shoulders. Suddenly all the things which do have colour fill him with joy, because the thought of colour no longer fills him with guilt for doubting the meaningless statement, 'the wind is green'.

So it will be for us when we stop trying to believe an impossible faith. Freed from the burden of trying to believe in a *supernatural* world, we shall find a new joy in the *natural* world and in human life.

2

Where is Now their God?

I have said that my 'conversion' to a genuine Christian faith of my own came about when I had the courage to say, 'I do not believe in God.' But how can I be a Christian if I do not believe in God? Doesn't it make me an atheist? Put that way, the question assumes that there is only one meaning to the word God and that we all know exactly what it is. But to ask, 'Do you believe in God?' is rather like asking, 'How long is a piece of string?' Show me the piece of string and I will tell you how long it is. Tell me what sort of God you have in mind and I will tell you whether I believe in him (or her? or it?). In my case I needed to be rid of one idea of God in order to make room for a new one.

From childhood I had accepted the traditional model of the Christian God, i.e. a supernatural person, beyond space and time, who is all-knowing, all-powerful, all-good, the creator and sustainer of the universe, and the proper object of human worship and obedience. For any believer in this sort of God there is a dilemma which cannot be avoided. By definition, he is beyond time and space, while we are limited to time and space. How then can we know anything about him? How can we know all the things listed earlier in this paragraph?

There are two approaches to this problem of gaining knowledge about God. Both have been used in compiling classical Christianity. The first, known as 'natural theology', says: we cannot reach God direct, so we must look for clues to his nature in the world around us. The second, known as 'revealed theology', says: we cannot reach outside time and space to God, but he does reach inside them to speak to us, if only we will listen.

These two methods have been argued about for hundreds of years. We shall look at a few examples of their use, and I will try to show why they can no longer be used today to make the claims to knowledge which they have been called upon to justify in the past.

Natural theology

The first alleged clue to God's existence to be found in the natural world is the sheer fact that *anything* exists. On the basis that 'nothing comes from nothing' it is reasonable to argue that there must have been some 'first cause' of the universe, and that is God.

I have never found this a convincing argument since, as the schoolboy put it, 'If God made everything, who made God?' To which we have to answer, 'No one made God, he is just there.' It seems to me as logical to say, 'No one made the universe, it is just there,' as it is to name God as the cause of the universe, and then have to say of God that 'No one made him, he is just there.' A more serious limitation, even for those who find the 'first cause' argument more helpful than I have, is that it gives no new information about God. All it does is to define one way to use the word 'God', namely: 'God = that which first caused the universe to come into being.' Nothing more than that. It gives no reason to apply to this 'God' any of the descriptions traditionally used of him, except creator. Even this term is misleading, because it conjures up all sorts of ideas about how creation might have happened. The definition of God as 'first cause' can tell us nothing about these things. It could apply equally to the 'Big Bang' myth of modern astrophysics, or to either of the creation stories in Genesis, or to any other theory of the origin of the universe.

A second alleged clue to God's existence is the pattern and order in the universe. Such a carefully ordered system cannot have come about by accident, the argument goes: it must have been designed for a purpose, and put in place to achieve some aim. A famous illustration puts it like this: if I am walking across the heath and find a stone, I might reasonably suppose that it came there by accident; but if I find a watch, with all its intricate cogs and wheels and mechanisms, I can only suppose that it was designed and made by an intelligent mind. And the universe – as we observe it – is more like the watch than the stone: it 'works' and therefore must have been planned and executed with a purpose. The same point was made more poetically in a hymn which we still sing:

> The spacious firmament on high,
> With all the blue ethereal sky,
> And spangled heavens, a shining frame,
> Their great Original proclaim.
> The unwearied sun from day to day
> Does his Creator's power display,

And publishes to every land
The works of an almighty hand.

This argument appeals to common sense and it *feels* conclusive. I can still remember my dismay when I was told that it does not prove anything! As a science under-graduate I was much comforted by this 'argument from design', as it is called. I happened to say this to a friend who was studying theology, and he broke the bad news: even if it be granted that the universe has a pattern and a purpose, what can we deduce from this? At most, that the universe had a designer. And what can we learn from that information? Only that the universe is designed, with a pattern and a purpose. Which is where we started! Even if the argument were to persuade us that the universe had a designer, *that is all that it could do*. It does not tell us whether it is a good design or a bad one, or whether ours is the only universe or one of many, or whether there was one planner or a design team. Most significantly it gives no grounds for claiming that the *designer* of the universe is the same person as the *maker* of it. Like the 'first cause' argument, the argument 'from design' can give us no information which we have not already put there our-selves. It gives us no reason to apply to the designer of the universe any of the divine attributes listed at the beginning of this chapter.

Emotionally I hung on to the design argument long after conceding that there was no intellectual force in it. And it was my emotional response, to a growing doubt that the universe really has a design, which finally tipped the balance against it: I can still admire the way in which the elements of nature interlock, but I can no longer accept that it is the result of a plan. For example, I can marvel that animals have so developed that they can breathe air; I cannot accept (as the old view required) that God made air the way he did *in order* that the animals could breathe. Nor can I accept any longer (as traditional faith requires) that a good and skilful God would have designed so much waste and violence into nature, 'red in tooth and claw'.

Heart and head are rarely in step when our deep-down assumptions are challenged. 'Conversion' comes when either the heart accepts what the head has long admitted, or when the head can finally justify a move which the heart has instinctively taken long before. In my own case the heart has been trailing the head by about twenty-five years! Be that as it may, a crucial and general principle has emerged from these two examples, which thinking heads need to ponder: *observations made within the natural world can give us no information about anything beyond the natural world.* They might lead us to imagine the existence of supernatural beings, but they can tell us nothing about them, not even whether they exist.

Revealed theology

We are bound to fail if we try to gain information about a supernatural God by our own efforts. What about the other route? Has such a God taken the initiative and told us about himself? This is the claim made for the books of the Bible, for the teachings of the creeds, and above all for the whole life of Jesus Christ. Let us take as an example the book of Genesis. Its opening chapters deal with matters which are pre-historical. No one was there to observe them. So, it is said, God has given the information direct, including both the facts and also the reasons and explanations for those facts. He has told us that he is a personal being; that he created the universe as a totally good thing; that he saw it begin to go wrong because one of his creatures misused the freewill he had been given; that God therefore had to intervene and destroy the whole earth by flood and start again with just one pair of each creature, etc. etc.

We are not concerned here with Genesis as a source of knowledge about the earth's beginnings, but as a source of knowledge about God. As such it has one fatal flaw: there is no way to test it. We can investigate all the human elements in the book. In theory, though probably not in practice, we could find out who wrote it and when, where they got their information and what they thought they were doing. If we could ask them, they might say (like Mohammed recording the Koran) that they were taking down divine dictation, or they might say that they were just recording ancient tribal stories. (On the traditional view, the latter would not prevent the work's being God's revelation. It has been held that writings can be divinely inspired even though it was not realized at the time.) The fact remains that the most we could know for certain would be the human history of the book. It may be that behind that human history was a guiding supernatural hand, whether or not the authors and editors were aware of it. We can never know. What we do know is that every jot and tittle of Genesis does have a human authorship and a human history. The God it portrays is a human creation, however inspired.

Another principle emerges: *Divine revelation (if it does*

exist) is always human at the point of delivery. In other words we are back with our first case: trying to get supernatural information from the human end of things.

That the Bible is a human writing, with no higher authority than we choose to give it on its own merits, is something which I have accepted since my student days, so there has been no change in my attitude towards it as a result of last summer's conversion. If anything, I have felt freer than before to appreciate the scriptures for the creative genius their writers display. I am aware, however, that challenging the authority of the Bible is the most sensitive issue in the church today. That is why it cannot be ducked. Discussions of other issues, such as the virgin birth and the resurrection of Jesus, are bedevilled (it is hardly too strong a word) by a refusal to admit the obvious: that the Bible contains truths, half-truths, untruths, good ideas, bad ideas, helpful ways of looking at things, and unhelpful ways. If I decide to call the Bible a divine revelation, which must therefore be free from error and contradiction, that is up to me. But I could just as well make the same claim for Shakespeare's plays, Tolkien's *Lord of the Rings*, or *Winnie the Pooh*. All are human books; all could have been written under divine inspiration, all have in fact been used in the pulpit to illustrate Christian teaching. The point is this: if there is a personal God beyond space and time, and if he has in fact chosen to use the Bible as a unique means of self-revelation, there is no means by which we can know that to be the case. At the point of delivery, alleged revelation is in fully human words and cannot be told apart from other human words. What makes the Bible unique in the Christian tradition is not its origins but the use it has been put to and the value which has been put upon it. And those have been human decisions which have given the Bible its authority and made it what it is.

At this point it may be objected that the written word is not the only, or even the most important, of the ways God makes himself known. Many people have had direct experience of God in their lives. This is certainly a common claim. In a recent discussion group, of both regular churchgoers and those who would not, I think, call themselves believers, members were asked to say something of their understanding of God. Without exception, they chose to speak of some experience which they felt was an encounter with God. What are we to make of this? There are three important points to be made.

First, it does not alter the fact that revelation is human at the point of delivery. All the members of the group described events which were fully human, which they themselves had experienced. They could only use the word 'God' to interpret those events because of ideas about God which they already held. The very form in which they experienced the events was probably shaped by the God-language they used to interpret it. This is a familiar finding. Popular catholic devotion centres largely on the virgin Mary, whose pictures and statues are found in all churches; so catholics report visions of the virgin. Protestant evangelicals never have such visions. The emotional centre of their religion is the Word of God, so they tend to report verbal messages (rather than visions) and think of them as coming direct from God (rather than through the saints). People with vaguer religious ideas than catholics and evangelicals report less clear religious experiences: a sense of peace, of light, of strength, etc. In every case the experience is described in the religious terms already to hand.

This does not disprove revelation. Each of the reported experiences might have had a supernatural origin, or a natural one. What I am saying is that there is no way, either in theory or practice, in which it would be possible to tell the difference. Such claims do not therefore prove that revelation takes place, only that some people experience certain events as revelation. And that is not at all the same thing.

Secondly, such an experience may modify the person's idea of God. This could be claimed as evidence that God not only communicates with us 'heart to heart' as it were, but also gives information about himself. I would say that it is an example of the way we all remake our own version of God in the light of our (human) experience. If you experience reassurance, and interpret this as God's action, then the giving of reassurance will be added to the qualities owned by your God. You will have had the experience; you will have done the adding to your own picture of God; nothing supernatural is required by what has happened.

The third point is this. Even those in the group who would not call themselves believers in the full Christian sense chose to speak of an *experience* rather than to talk about any *theory of God*, say as creator. This encourages me to think that 'using God practically' (if I may so put it) is more important to people than 'thinking about him theoretically'. In other words, allowing a much wider understanding of what 'God' means need not harm religious experience but may even enhance it. I can remember saying in my liberal days that I was more certain of God's care for me than of his existence. Now I would put that rather differently: I can still benefit from using God religiously, without believing in him as an objective and active supernatural person.

Faith without a supernatural God

So far we have looked at problems raised by faith in a supernatural God. They do not force us into disbelief, although they may be one element in allowing us to recognize it. My own view is that what I call genuine faith is not a thing we can choose. It has been called a gift. That is certainly what it feels like. My basic beliefs may change from time to time, but that is not something within my control. The most that I can do is (consciously or sub-consciously) resist acknowledging the change. It is quite different with what, as a scientist, I would call a working hypothesis. That is something which I can choose and alter at will. I doubt, looking back, whether I have ever really *believed* in the traditional God. Certainly I do not now. But for nearly all my life I have used him as a working hypothesis: if such a God were to exist, then such and such would follow. Now I am working from the opposite end: suppose that such a God does not exist independently, but is just a human projection, then what?

At one level, surprisingly little changes! We have seen already that we can have no access to information outside this natural world. So what have people done in the past when they have claimed to have knowledge about God? They have described God as an ideal (superhuman) person. They have said, God must have to an infinite degree all the good qualities of life, and in no degree at all any of the restricting qualities. Hence the positive labels: all-good, all-loving, all-mighty, all-knowing, all-wise, etc.; and the negative labels: immortal (free from death), invisible (free from intrusion), eternal (free from time), impassible (free from suffering), etc. They have not learned these things about God from any outside information. They have worked it out for themselves. They have said, If there is a God worthy of the name, then this must be the sort of God he is.

Now I have decided to change my use of the term God. Instead of referring it to a supernatural being, I shall apply it to the sum of all my values and ideals in life. To describe my new God I must list those values. What are they? Some are positive things like goodness, love, power (rightly used), knowledge, wisdom, etc. and some are negative, such as freedom from the fear and tyranny of death, of suffering, etc. So my new God sounds remarkably like my old one – for the simple reason that the description has been built up in the same way. Ever since we embraced just one God, he has always been in fact the sum of all our ideals. The only difference now is that we are able (should be able) to accept that this is what he is, without having to claim for him an independent supernatural existence. The Greeks and Romans made their values into different divine beings, such as Aphrodite and Venus for love. The first Christians were called atheists for refusing to acknowledge that they had personal existence. We are now saying that, like those ancient gods, ours too has no independent existence. And we shall be called atheists too – just as unfairly.

The making of gods is found in the Bible as well. It was one of Israel's taunts of her pagan neighbours that they worshipped gods which they had made with their own hands. There are many examples, but the finest is this piece of satire on the idol-worshipper:

> He plants a cedar and the rain nourishes it. Then it becomes fuel for a man; he takes a part of it and warms himself, he kindles a fire and bakes bread; also he makes a god and worships it, he makes it a graven image and falls down before it. Half of it he burns in the fire; over the half he eats flesh, he roasts meat and is satisfied; also he warms himself and says, 'Aha, I am warm, I have seen the fire!' And the rest of it he makes into a god, his idol; he falls down to it and worships it; he prays to it and says, 'Deliver me, for thou art my god!' (Isa. 44.14b–17).

What the writer of this splendid piece failed to realize was how close his own case was to that of the pagan whom he was lampooning. The idol-worshipper had constructed his god with wood; our author had made his God out of words: that was the only difference. Our author might be parodied:

> He sets out language and usage fosters it. Then it becomes a tool for man; he takes part of it and orders his life with words such as fire and bread; also he makes God and worships him, he makes a verbal image and falls down before it. Half of it he uses in the day-to-day business of running the house and home and is satisfied; also he writes poetry and says, 'Aha, I can write, I have seen the light!' And the rest of it he makes into a God,

his idol; he falls down to it and worships it; he prays to it and says, 'Deliver me, for thou art my God!'

The significant difference between the two is that the pagan knew what he was doing. He knew very well that he was making a religious symbol out of earthly materials. But our author did *not* realize what he himself was doing. He believed that the God whose mental image and messages he had formed in his mind *really was 'out there'* giving orders and making promises, but that was not the case. He was a created God, made – not with human hands – but with human thoughts out of human words. Isaiah's God and the Christian God are just as much human creations as the idols of Canaan. So by saying that God is my own creation – my ideals personified – I am doing nothing new, but only acknowledging what has always been the case.

We still personify some virtues even now and in England. 'Duty calls!' 'Loyalty demands. . .' 'Love conquers all!' But we no longer think of duty, loyalty and love as actually being 'out there' somewhere, calling and demanding and conquering. In the same way, we can still speak of God's calling us or guiding us, without having to imagine him 'out there' as a person. We may even still speak of God as creator in a way that has meaning: our ultimate values are what give order and perspective and motivation to all that we do. It does therefore make sense to speak of them as 'creating' our lives, making them what they are. It has more meaning for me to say that my life is created by my values, than by some unimaginable first cause of the universe ten billion years ago.

Another advantage to this way of thinking about God

is its flexibility. Our values change. Even within my own lifetime, the relative value given to the rights of animals, the care of the environment, the concept of equal rights, and a number of other issues, has changed enormously. This sort of change was hard to fit into our religious beliefs when we had a model of God as a person with fixed and known qualities. Our value-god is much more flexible. We can change the qualities we emphasize in her to reflect our own changing concerns. (There! We've just done it!) This changing of standards and ideals is nothing new. A hundred and fifty years ago people were drummed out of the Church of England for daring to suggest that God does not punish sinners eternally in hell fire. Nowadays you hit the headlines if you do preach this doctrine. I am not saying which is right or wrong; only pointing out that our understanding of God, and the values he represents, has always been a changeable thing. The difference now is that we can (and probably ought to) admit this and make the changes more quickly.

I return finally to the questions with which we began: 'Do you believe in God? Are you not an atheist?' The answer is, 'Yes, I do believe in God, and one of the things I believe about God is that he does not exist.' This is not just my being clever. A very important point is being made. Our view of religion as a human creation – let us call it Christian humanism – still stands firmly in the Christian tradition and sees itself as a legitimate heir to the New Testament. We still find value in the Christian vocabulary, including the word God, and in the Christian stories, especially those of Jesus. A secular humanist, an atheist, has no place for such things. That does not mean that for us it is simply, 'business as usual'. If we are to take seriously the non-supernatural form of Christianity which I am commending, then the emphasis of religion shifts from heaven to earth, from the next world to this one, and from dogma to spirituality and ethics. But religion still has an important place in human life.

3

Our Saviour Jesus Christ

Certain key teachings need to be restated in a quite new way if we are to have a Christianity without the supernatural. We have already looked at the first of these: belief in God as the creator and sustainer of the universe. In this chapter we come to the heart of the Christian gospel: that God became human in the person of Jesus Christ who died to save us from sin and death.

To speak of a saviour implies that there is something we need saving from. That 'something' is given by Christians the name 'sin'. But what is sin? 'What is sin?' was the title of the only essay I failed to complete when I was a student at theological college. (I leave you to draw your own conclusions from that fact!) The thing which interests me now is that I can still remember the opening sentence of what I did write. I said, *Sin is a theological invention.* This shows that my leanings towards religion as a human creation go a long way back. It also helps to explain why I never finished the essay: I was trying to cope with a humanist view of sin in a framework of supernatural religion. No wonder I could not do it! Now that I can see that both sin and God-the-saviour are human inventions, maybe I shall have more success.

Christian stories in the past

Views of sin, like all things human, run in fashions. The great fear and anxiety of one generation is hardly given a thought by another. So naturally the qualities looked for in a saviour-from-sin run in fashions as well. For the first few hundred years of our era, when the foundation stones of Christian doctrine were being laid, the great fear was extinction. The anxiety of the age was that earthly death meant total oblivion, and that was the fate from which any religion had to offer a way of escape. The Christian response to this fear took the form of a drama in four acts:

1. God made humanity in his own image, and part of what it meant to be in God's image was that humanity shared as a gift what God himself had by nature: immortality.

2. As a result of human sin, the image became marred, and so the gift of immortality was lost. Only by restoring the divine image in the human race could the gift be conferred anew.

3. In Jesus Christ, God himself took on a human life and so renewed the perfect divine image and the gift of eternal life in a single human. This was triumphantly proved by the defeat of death in the resurrection of Jesus.

4. Potentially that renewal was achieved in every human being; to make it actual, a person needed to be baptized. This made them a sharer of Christ's new

humanity and therefore also of his divinity and of his immortality.

'He shared our human life in order that we might share his divine life,' was a common slogan in those days, summing up both the method and purpose of the saviour. It was an important principle that Jesus should be both 100% God and also 100% human. If his divinity had been at all suspect, then his ability to renew the divine image and so confer the gift of immortality upon the human race would have been fatally harmed. If he were not fully human, then whatever aspect of humanity he lacked would remain unredeemed. All the doctrinal battles of the first five centuries were fought to ensure that these three basic criteria should be fulfilled: that Jesus should be fully God, fully man, and a fully integrated single person.

By the Middle Ages, the fashion had changed. The message for which the early church had fought so hard was taken for granted, so much so that it was commonly believed that the human soul was by nature immortal. The major consequence of sin was no longer thought of as loss of life but as punishment for wickedness. So the great anxiety was no longer that death would mean extinction, but that death would mean an eternity in hellfire. The church responded by shifting the emphasis from the birth of Jesus to the death of Jesus, because this was seen as the key to escape from punishment. The script of the play had been completely re-written and now looked like this:

1. Humanity has been disobedient (sinful) from the

first and must be punished or make recompense. God's honour and holiness do not permit this to be ignored.

2. In Jesus Christ, God the son lived a perfectly obedient (sinless) human life and so did not deserve death as a punishment.

3. By offering his perfect life (human and divine) freely and willingly on the cross, Jesus paid the debt of the whole human race.

4. This means that God can forgive human sins without offending his honour and holiness, and he does this through the sacraments of the church.

This theory again required that Jesus be both fully human and fully divine. Only if he were fully divine would he be capable of living the sinless life and only if the gift were of God's own life would it be of sufficient worth. But only if he were fully human would he be qualified to make the payment: humanity had sinned and so humanity had to pay off the debt.

Today the situation has changed again. Not many people live in mortal fear of roasting in hell. (Though there *is* still great anxiety on the part of conservative Christians, not for themselves, but for their unbelieving friends and relatives. This is one reason why these scare-mongering doctrines need to be challenged.) What we do find today is a lot of unresolved guilt and an inability of people to forgive *themselves*. This reflects a longstanding negative attitude by the church towards human worth, and is looked at in the next chapter. The greatest overall anxiety today would seem to be that there is no meaning in life, no ultimate purpose to anything. A sense of lostness. (Sometimes this is reflected in a return to the old fear that death means extinction. The insistence of some conservative Christians on the physical resurrection may be an aspect of this. But the real sickness of our age is the sense of aimlessness.)

The challenge to Christians of all points of view today is this: do we re-tell the Christian good news so that it effectively meets today's generation at its point of need? Or do we try to induce in people the old anxieties of the past, to which we have pre-packaged Christian remedies? I have no doubt that it is the first of these choices which we have to take. This being so, radical Christians, who are less bound than others to past slogans and beliefs, should be at a positive advantage.

It may come as a surprise to you that Christian teaching has changed over the years and can be so easily identified as belonging to a particular time or even a particular writer. We have been trained to believe that Christian truth is unchanging. But think for a moment of other areas of life. I am no great musician but, if I hear an unfamiliar piece of music on the radio, I can normally tell at once whether it is from the baroque, classical, romantic or modern period. I have only a slight knowledge of art history, but faced with an unfamiliar painting I could tell a renaissance Italian work from a Russian ikon or a French impressionist. In the case of a very distinctive style I might even be able to name the artist – Degas perhaps, or Renoir. Going 'down market' a bit, think of Hollywood historical dramas. The scene may be ancient Rome, or King Arthur's Camelot, but the hairstyles and costumes tell you at once in which decade of the present century the film was made. Religious teaching gives away its age just as surely.

The New Testament faces of Jesus

In the case of the earliest Christian books – those in the New Testament – we have a unique situation. Although they were all written at more or less the same time, they come from different places and show us independent responses to Jesus Christ. They date from a time before there was a single church with an agreed interpretation of events. (That is why so many quite different ideas have subsequently been able to claim support from the New Testament.) Look at St Paul, who is widely thought of as the co-founder of Christianity and whose letters are the earliest Christian writings we have. He tells us nothing about the earthly life of Jesus before the day of his death, and almost nothing about that last twenty-four hours. For Paul, it is the Lord Jesus Christ who matters, a mystical person who was raised from the dead, whose body is the Christian community, and whose spirit lives in all Christians. If we had to rely on St Paul for information, we should not know that Jesus ever told a parable, nor that he ever performed a miracle. By contrast consider St Mark, normally thought to have written the earliest of the Gospels. He tells us nothing of Jesus *except* his earthly life. He gives us selected stories between his baptism in the river Jordan and the discovery of his empty tomb, and there stops abruptly – almost in mid-sentence. If we had to rely on St Mark for information, we should not know whether Jesus ever met up with his disciples again, nor whether his religious movement survived his death. Each

New Testament writer gives us his own Jesus, and once you know them they are easily identified.

For most of its two-thousand-year history, the church in each age has had what we can now see is its own composite picture of Jesus. And each age, looking back over the biblical books and other Christian texts, has found its own Jesus there. This process was quite unconscious. Only in the past couple of hundred years, with the rise of historical research, has it been realized what was going on. As a reaction, the attempt has been made to draw a distinction between two characters. One is the Jesus of history, the actual figure we might have met by the Sea of Galilee, and who must be open to investigation by historians. The other is the Christ of faith, the figure proclaimed by the church as saviour of the world, who is liable to change in changing circumstances. It has to be said that this venture, the 'quest for the historical Jesus', has not been a success. The starting point was to take St Paul's Lord as the basic 'Christ of faith' and St Mark's itinerant preacher as the basic 'historical Jesus'. Careful comparison of the four Gospels showed how certain qualities of the 'Christ of faith' seemed to have been read back into the life of the 'historical Jesus'. Much painstaking work led to a whole spate of biographies. The earliest, which opened up the entire field, was the *Life of Jesus* by D.F. Strauss, published in 1835. The most recent serious example I have seen is *The Founder of Christianity* by C.H. Dodd, coming a century and a half later. The trouble with these books is that, like the Hollywood costume dramas, they tell us far more about their author and the time they were written than about the historical character of Jesus. In all ages we look down the well of history and see our own reflection.

In the light of the failure of 'the quest', there are three options. The conservative one is to deny the distinction; to go back to a pre-critical reading of the texts and insist that the Jesus of history simply is the Christ of faith exactly as portrayed by the evangelists and Paul. The liberal response is to deny the failure and to continue patient historical and literary research. The radical answer is to accept the distinction and the failure and to say that it does not matter! Who needs the historical Jesus? Paul got on very well without him, and the four evangelists were each quite content to construct their own version of him. Why cannot we do the same? All the New Testament writers presented their readers with the Christ they needed. The church fathers of the first five centuries created a Christ who fulfilled their needs in a saviour. The mediaeval scholars did the same, and so did the sixteenth-century reformers and all other theologians since. So why break the habits of a life-time? Let us do exactly what all previous generations have done and create our own Jesus. The only difference will be that what they did unconsciously we shall be doing openly and knowingly.

Let us be clear what we are saying. We have no choice in the matter. Even if we wanted to, we could not study the historical character called Jesus of Nazareth, and decide on the evidence whether to accept him as our saviour. The evidence simply is not there. The four Gospels are not reports about a man's life. They are proclamations that Jesus is Lord. At first glance, or even after careful study, they may appear to be 'lives of Jesus'. But they are not. The lesson, the hard and still-to-be-taken-in lesson, of the failure of the quest for the historical Jesus is just this: St Mark may appear to talk only about the earthly life of Jesus, but he is in fact presenting us with the Lord Jesus Christ every bit as much as St Paul is. And so is Matthew, and Luke, and John. Each of them – like each generation of Christians since – has confessed him as saviour, and then applied to him the necessary qualities to do the job. That may sound awful, but it is what has happened. And it has worked!

Let us take an example. For reasons now lost to us, the first Christians were convinced that Jesus was the Christ. But he came from Nazareth, and the scriptures foretold that the Christ would be born in Bethlehem. How did each of the evangelists deal with this? Mark ignores it altogether. John refers to the discrepancy (John 7.41f.) but leaves it unresolved, preferring to draw his readers' attention away from Jesus' earthly origins to his heavenly ones (cf. John 1.14; 3.13; 16.28). Matthew says that Jesus' parents lived at Bethlehem up to the time of his birth, but moved to Nazareth later to avoid persecution by the Herod family (Matt. 2.1, 22f.). Luke says that the family lived in Nazareth, and were only in Bethlehem at the time of the birth because of the census (Luke 1.26; 2.4–7). The point I am making is this: none of the evangelists believed that Jesus was the Christ because they knew he was born in Bethlehem. They thought he must have been born in Bethlehem because that was one of the criteria for being the Christ *which they already believed on other grounds*. So they made Jesus fit the criteria of their saviour. Naturally.

Remaking Jesus Christ today

The work of remaking Christian doctrine has to go on. It has always been thus. We saw earlier an example from the fourth century. In order to be saviour (as then understood), Jesus had to be divine. But this teaching was in danger of breaking another standard belief of the time: that God cannot suffer. One group of Christians kept the balance by saying that although Jesus was divine, he was not 'of one substance' with God the father. Another group insisted that to be fully God he must be 'of one substance' with the father. They won, and the phrase is in the creed to this day. The doctrine is not in the Bible. But the church of the day said it was a necessary qualification for the saviour to have, so they made it a part of the Christian faith.

This may seem shocking, but we have to get away from the idea that Christian teaching about Jesus fell out of the sky ready-made. The creed just as much as the Bible has 'made on earth' written all over it. Made and re-made as circumstances required. It does not describe a timeless situation in a supernatural world. It sets out the belief-needs of a particular group of people at a particular time. We cannot be bound by it. We must be as innovative as those early Christians who wrote it.

Even if what I have just said is accepted, it may seem that to present a picture of Jesus which would fit in with a non-supernatural version of Christianity would be impossible. But if we go back to some of the key characteristics of Jesus in the Gospels, we need be no more selective than anyone else has been in order to produce a reasonable and usable ikon.

39

1. He does not teach by giving direct information about God. He tells stories and lets people draw their own conclusions. He reacts to questions by asking more questions.

2. He challenges the religious norms of the day. He breaks the sabbath, attacks the food laws, ignores the purity code.

3. He sits lightly to the moral conventions of the day. He keeps company with sinners and denounces the hypocrisy of the upright.

4. He calls his hearers to a completely new attitude to life: to turn around, to trust, to love, to forgive, and not to judge.

I am not claiming that Jesus in the Gospels did not believe in God as an objective reality. That would be absurd. I am saying that there is much in the Gospel teaching of Jesus which loses none of its force, which indeed gains added weight, if there is not an objective God. More than that, I am saying that much in the attitude of Jesus in the Gospels encourages bold innovation. To read the text so as to bring this side of Jesus into focus is quite proper. And I dare say it conflicts less with the evidence than does that more common public-school portrayal of Jesus as the upright citizen and promoter of the status quo.

Maybe. But can this radical reading of the text give us a saviour? If it is true that our world today is afflicted by a fear of aimlessness, can this Jesus help, this Jesus who is just words on a page, whose objective existence we deny? The lost sheep needed a real shepherd to come and rescue him. The lost coin needed a real housewife to search it out. Do we not need a real saviour, a God who really is 'out there' and able to reach into our world and find us and bring us safely home? Perhaps it would be nice if that were the case, but we have seen the reasons why we cannot accept such a picture as literally true. In the previous chapter we saw that it is simply not possible to have information about such a supernatural being even if he did exist. In this chapter we have seen that the picture we have of Jesus is a human creation. Any power he has is that which we ourselves supply by using him as a focus and symbol for our own energies. But is this really such a loss? Do I really want to be like a lifeless coin, someone else's plaything to lose and find? Do I even want to be like a helpless lamb, dependent on a shepherd? Such metaphors do less than justice to the creative genius of human beings. Traditional religion has encouraged a wrong kind of dependency and devaluing of ourselves by using them.

St Luke sets alongside these parables of the lost sheep and the lost coin that of the lost son (more often called the prodigal son; see Luke 15). In this story the realization of his plight and the initiative to do something about it come from the young man himself. This is a better role-model for us. We are to work out our own salvation. The figure of Jesus will indeed help in this – providing an example, a symbol, a focus for our efforts – and without such support we cannot help ourselves. His role of saviour is therefore real and necessary, but the energy will come from us and there is no need for Jesus to exist ouside the text and our reading of it. Like the lost son in the story, we shall 'come to ourselves' and find our own way. It is true that the world has no meaning in itself. But we have the power to give it meaning by the value and values we put on it. Traditional religion devalues this world and its experiences, by contrasting their transience with the 'solid joys and lasting treasures' of the unseen world to come. We shall find our way when we give meaning to the here and now by our own commitment to the Christian values of love, joy, peace, etc. Jesus is our saviour when he focusses that commitment.

This is not quite so revolutionary to Christian thought as may appear. In the early days of the church there was a strong element of teaching which was totally negative about the present world and saw salvation in terms of escape from it. This extreme view never became official teaching. The official line of the church has always been the salvation *of* the world rather than salvation *from* the world. The physical resurrection has been seen as an important safeguard of this principle (despite the extreme difficulty of giving any precise meaning to that doctrine). What I am proposing simply takes this one stage further. Not salvation *from* this world, nor even salvation *of* this world (in the sense of its transfer lock-stock-and-barrel to some better place) but salvation *in* this world and *for* this world. And the life-loving, life-affirming character who is one of the faces of Jesus in the Gospels, is a worthy focus of such a view on life.

The uniqueness of Jesus

Many will be concerned that by this approach we lose the claim to the uniqueness of Jesus, but that is in fact a gain.

One of the great challenges to the church today is the existence of other faiths on our doorstep. Is it possible to affirm our own tradition without denying theirs? The claim to Christian uniqueness hampers genuine dialogue and if we have found a legitimate form of Christianity which avoids this problem, so much the better.

I sometimes put the question this way: Jews, Christians and Muslims all claim to worship the God of Abraham. Yet Christians say they worship God who is a holy trinity while the other two faiths deny this doctrine. Which then is more misleading: to say that we all worship the same God, or that we worship different Gods? World peace in the next century could depend upon finding the right answer to that question. If we believed there were an actual being 'out there' called God, then it would make sense – and indeed be essential – to ask which of the many versions of God is closest to the truth. Only one could be right. But if we admit that the religions (and the branches within each one) are parallel human developments, and each has created its own God, with some common elements and some independent ones, then it is much easier to be positive about all of them. We are not forced to call one right and another wrong, any more than we do with traditions of, say, art.

A familiar parable (attempting to allow some descriptive truth to all the faiths) likens the world religions to a number of blind men feeling the different parts of an elephant and each bringing his own contribution to the whole picture. On our view, a better analogy would be a number of people looking at clouds changing shape in the sky and saying how the different shapes appeared to them. In this second case there is no absolute truth by which the different offerings can be judged. Each carries its own truth. Central to our Christian humanist picture will be the idea that in Jesus the ultimate value of all human life is affirmed. 'God in Christ' will come to mean that Jesus provides a unique focus for all human ideals, but not in a way which denies the other religious traditions.

4

The Holy Human Spirit

If there is a pointer anywhere in the mainstream Christian tradition to the kind of Christian humanism which I am commending, then it is in the doctrine of the Holy Spirit. Whitsunday – the feast of the Holy Spirit in the Christian calendar – is a celebration of the 'earthing' of religion, and very heavy weather the church has made of it over the years!

The go-between church

This is not surprising. Organized religion has relied upon there being a gulf between heaven and earth to give it a purpose: the church's main reason for existing is to bridge this gap, to provide a means of communication between God and his world. In the one direction it carries all official messages *from* God. These are in the Bible (which is the church's book) and in the solemnly ratified teaching of the great bishops and Christian teachers, summarized in the creeds. In the other direction it is the official channel of effective prayer *to* God, through its ceaseless round of worship. Above all is this focussed in holy communion, where we offer our sacrifice of praise and thanksgiving to God, and he nourishes us with the body and blood of his

45

son Jesus Christ. All this machinery for bridging the gap between God and his world centres on the church.

Nothing is so calculated to upset this cosy arrangement as the news that the gap does not exist! Yet this is precisely the message of Whitsunday (see Acts 2). The Holy Spirit has been poured out on all flesh in fulfilment of Joel's prophecy. What had seemed unique to Jesus – the bringing together of God and man – is now made completely democratic. Old and young, male and female, slave and free: all have received the Spirit. No longer is God to be the object of our distant gaze. No longer is the Holy Spirit a supernatural agent directing just a small number of specially chosen priests or prophets or kings. That old system died with Jesus on the cross. Its end was symbolized in the rending of the temple veil from top to bottom. God has been democratized. God is now present in the hearts and lives of ordinary people as they go about their everyday business. Wonderful news!

You might have thought that such a revolution would spell the end of the church. When God was thought of as a distant powerful person to be placated or asked for help, then the church was in business. But now, in the post-Whitsun world, that idea has been replaced by the thought of God as an ever-present reality, giving meaning and direction to all our lives here and now. Surely the church is out of a job? As the prophet Jeremiah had put it hundreds of years earlier: 'No longer shall each man teach his neighbour and each his brother saying, "Know the Lord," for they shall all know me, from the least of them to the greatest, says the Lord' (31.34). But just the opposite happened. So far from spelling the end of the church, Whitsun is commonly spoken of as being the church's birthday. How is this? It is because the full implications of the doctrine of the Holy Spirit have never been accepted. They have been evaded in two ways.

The first way has been to sidestep the absolute idea that God has become earthed. By developing the doctrine of the trinity, the church has managed to retain its distant father-god away in heaven, while still paying lip-service to the ever-present spirit-god here on earth. A thorough-going Christian humanism, which is the logical consequence of the belief that God is in every one of us through the Spirit, has thus been avoided.

The second evasion is based on a discrepancy in St Luke's account of the first Whitsun in Acts 2. The explanation of the events of that day, given by St Peter in his sermon, proclaims the fulfilment of Joel: 'I will pour out my spirit upon all flesh.' But the description of the events says that only on the twelve apostles did the Spirit fall. As the story of Acts unfolds, we find that it is only in response to the preaching, the baptism, and the laying on of hands of the apostles (or their authorized representatives) that the Spirit comes to others.

Putting these two things together meant that in practice little changed. There was still a distant God, even though the gap had been bridged by the Holy Spirit. And the apostles – succeeded in time by the church which they embodied – were the sole channels of that Spirit to the rest of humanity. Holy baptism, confirmation, holy communion: these became the means whereby the Holy Spirit came into the lives of ordinary men and women. And these sacraments were administered by and through the church. God was in his heaven, and he dealt with the world through his spirit *in the church*. And in effect, even if not in theory, that meant the clergy. Just like the old Jewish system. All had changed and all had remained the same!

The holy human spirit

The time has come to challenge this system. It is ironic that I, who do not for a moment take literally the story of the first Whitsun, am pleading for the message of the story to be taken very seriously indeed. Whereas the church, which appears to be committed to a realistic acceptance of the story, consistently refuses to hear the message! The idea that the Holy Spirit is a supernatural force invading this world (with or without wind and fire), and the idea of God the father as a supernatural person somewhere beyond the realms of time and space, have got to go. There are many reasons for this.

First, because they are becoming impossible for many people to find any meaning in. Thousands of people in the church, and millions outside it, are looking for a new way to give meaning to our human lives. While the church clings to these outdated ways of speaking, it will be unable to speak to this generation. We should have heeded Alexander Pope nearly three centuries ago:

Know then thyself, presume not God to scan,
The proper study of mankind is man.

Even on a traditional Christian outlook this should make sense: it is precisely by looking to what is noblest and best in our human spirits that we should discover the Holy

Spirit shed abroad in our hearts, and so come by the only knowledge of God which we can properly have.

Secondly (and paradoxically), we should challenge the doctrine of a supernatural spirit because a vulnerable minority of people do find it all too easy to believe in. This makes them easy prey to all sorts of deceivers and claimants to special powers. Until the church firmly distances itself from all such claims, it cannot bring its long and deep spiritual experience to help the weak and to challenge the pretended claims of religious sects and occult organizations. All too often, conservative churches look like rivals to these groups in the same market place, rather than the bringers of a totally different outlook on life, which should be the Christian gospel.

Thirdly, it is to be opposed because of what I call the 'Heads God wins; tails we lose!' syndrome. One of the greatest sources of illness in our society is the low esteem in which people hold themselves. Time and again the chief task of counsellors and therapists is to help us develop a positive attitude to ourselves. A religion which constantly degrades the human, and says that we can do nothing worthwhile except with this supernatural spirit, is psychologically harmful.

Fourthly, and leading on from this, calling on the supernatural has the effect of devaluing and downgrading all natural talent. A classic example of this is in the field of medicine. There was a recent Christian healing mission in London which must have cost hundreds of thousands of pounds, with little evidence of benefits to health. If a quarter of that money had been spent on conventional medical techniques, not only would the health gains have been far greater, the skills of the medical staff would have been affirmed. Of course people receive great comfort and genuine healing at Christian 'homes of healing': but it is the devotion and skill of the staff and the positive attitude of all concerned which accounts for this. We should be giving a positive boost to this power of the human spirit, not denying it in the name of supernatural powers.

I hope I have given enough examples to make my point. St John says that Jesus promised his disciples that the spirit would lead them into all truth. The truth into which the church is now being led is the radical Christian humanism which is the most obvious consequence of its own teaching about the Holy Spirit. Let us set aside the old supernatural beliefs, which in many ways still tie Christianity to its pre-Whitsuntide past, and take seriously Jesus' words according to St Luke, that the kingdom of God is within us and among us.

The Christian devaluing of the purely human has been so widespread over the years that we are bound to ask, What will be the practical effects of moving from the Holy Spirit in the human to the wholly human spirit? Will it not mean a relapse into selfish and self-centred lives? Certainly not. We can already see ways in which organizations with no formal religious basis are in the forefront of outward-looking and humanitarian causes: Oxfam, Amnesty International, Greenpeace, and many others. The environmental groups in particular give evidence of what can only be called religious and evangelistic zeal for their cause. I am not saying that a Christian humanist would be bound to join or even to support all these groups. I draw attention to them as examples of the commitment and unselfish fervour of which the human spirit is capable. This is not to deny that humans are also guilty of the most horrid atrocities: only that the presence or absence of traditional religious faith makes little apparent difference to whether the good or bad face of the human spirit prevails.

It is hardly an exaggeration to say that at the present time the moral and political values held by most English Christians are held in spite of, rather than because of, traditional Christian doctrine. I began this book with a political example. Living in a social democracy, we condemn dictatorship wherever it occurs. Yet our religious picture of God is of a dictator above all dictators: *High and mighty, King of kings, Lord of lords, the only Ruler of princes.* This example from the Book of Common Prayer (Morning and Evening Prayer) is extreme, but makes the point well for just that reason. Human rights are another widely accepted political and moral principle which have no basis at all in traditional Christianity. Quite the reverse. Men and women are regarded as rebellious creatures who deserve nothing but eternal damnation, and only by the grace of God does any of us escape this well-deserved fate. It is in spite of, not because of, our received doctrine that Christians have been in the forefront of social and political reform. Christian humanism will mean a revaluing of the human and the this-worldly. Leaving behind much of the baggage of past doctrine can only make this easier. And where things from the tradition are useful and inspiring, then (as in the past) we shall use them and benefit by them.

God in Us

Prayer and worship

Practising Christians are going to ask, What about prayer and worship? If God is not in his heaven, what on earth (!) is the purpose of praying in this new human-centred religion? The negative part of the answer is that people have largely stopped praying already, at least in public. Even where belief in God has not been lost entirely, belief in a God who actually interferes in worldly affairs has virtually gone. The government reaction to a water-shortage is not to pray for rain but to install domestic water meters. And one of the most popular religious opinions heard by the clergy is, 'You do not have to go to church to be a Christian.' To find the positive part of the answer, we need to look to where praying is still done, and found helpful by those who do it. We must ask what the activities labelled as prayer really are, and what human needs they are fulfilling. In my own mind I am clear that to reject the supernatural does not mean having to reject the spiritual as a real dimension to my life.

My own prayer has three main elements: the daily prayers of the church, normally read publicly but alone; Sunday worship with the congregation in which holy communion has a central place; and quiet times of reflection on my own. Since I acknowledged to myself that I do not actually believe there is anyone 'out there' listening to me, I have been surprised that it has not made the slightest difference to my prayers. I suppose that I must have sub-consciously accepted that I was talking to myself long before admitting it consciously. Yet I did and still do find the exercise of prayer helpful. Why is this?

The daily prayers are a useful discipline and serve to

'anchor the day fore and aft', as it were. Sunday worship provides fellowship with other Christians. In both cases, the use of familiar texts – hymns, prayers, Bible, etc. – helps me to feel that I belong. They give me a place in a tradition which stretches back and forward in time as well as sideways to my contemporaries. There is a problem in public worship when very often the words of the service say things which I think are not just old-fashioned but plain wrong. I mentioned this in the first chapter, together with the dangers of using a running translation to oneself. For myself, the answer at present is to use familiar ancient texts where one is hardly conscious of the words at all. Forms of prayer and worship which emphasize the personal aspect of God are clearly less helpful. This is why Christian humanists are likely to find the more detached older style of worship easier to cope with than charismatic and informal services. Fully choral Prayer Book services are the best for me at the present time.

Music can be a great help in making words acceptable for worship. People love to sing old hymns whose words, if they read and studied them, they would agree to be the most appalling nonsense. This is a common cause of anguish among clergy who vainly try to improve their flocks' taste in these matters. I am suggesting this well-known fact can be turned to advantage. The Nicene creed, for example, can hardly be said with full understanding by anyone these days. And few who do understand it could honestly say they believe it. But when set to music and sung as an act of allegiance to a tradition, the creed can be a powerful force for good. I heard someone the other day refer to the creeds as the 'rugger songs of the church'. This unlikely analogy does not refer to their

God in Us

contents but to their use: just as rugby players are bound together by certain commonly used songs (whose words are quite irrelevant to the purpose!), so are Christians bound together by chanting words hallowed by long use.

Christian humanists set aside the possibility of supernatural intervention in answer to prayer. This does not mean that when praying for other people we exclude the possibility of 'doing some good'. The very fact that I care enough to spend time praying for someone may bring some benefit where the person concerned knows about it. I am also open to the idea that in some natural (but as yet unexplained) way, the 'power of positive thought' can affect people and situations. Public intercession can be a way of both expressing a community's need, and evoking a response to it. In extreme cases this can be used as a form of blackmail, even – or maybe especially – in churches which place much store by God's answering prayer. Persistent prayers for children's work volunteers can put great moral pressure on members of a congregation. So can prayers for money. Public prayers are thus fully explicable in terms of the humans involved in them. The prayers both focus their shared concerns and encourage them to respond to these concerns. I strongly disapprove of the blackmail element in some evangelical prayers. I cite the example to underline the point that no supernatural agency is needed to explain a usefulness in this particular form of the activity we call prayer.

I have said that rejecting the supernatural (a word, by the way, not found in the Bible or the creeds) does not mean rejecting the spiritual. The two great sacraments of baptism and communion need not therefore lose their power by the shift of emphasis to this world. Indeed, this

54

is the sacramental principle: that water and bread, the staples of physical life, should also symbolize our spiritual life. Christening is already a largely 'secularized' ceremony in the hearts and minds of the English people. Zealous clergy of recent years have stressed that baptism is joining the church, and have tightened up the entry qualifications. It is a surer instinct which uses the old familiar name for the service, and makes it a welcome not only into the church but into the family and the wider society which the church serves.

The communion service is the regular remaking of the church community at two levels. First, each individual makes a personal renewal of commitment to the Christian values and draws strength from the tradition. This is central to the piety of the Church of England and explains the longing for the 'quiet eight o'clock service'. Here each worshipper is left alone with his or her own thoughts and prayers, and 'making my communion' is a deeply personal spiritual experience. Such a view of communion has been unfashionable for some years but is of great importance. Secondly, the fellowship of the local church is built up. Changes in styles of worship, intended to bring out this aspect, have not been entirely successful. They have destroyed the individual piety without creating the corporate. Having the priest face the people and making them all shake hands during the service will not, after all, turn an essentially individual experience into a fellowship. Something more like a harvest supper – with a full if simple meal and community singing – is perhaps needed for this human togetherness to be achieved. Such an occasion (the word service hardly seems suitable) could not be combined with the idea of 'making my communion'. It would be a quite different thing. But one of the advantages of a humanistic approach to worship is that it offers much more flexibility. We do not have to cram all the possible meanings of the communion into each gathering of the congregation.

The Church of England's teaching on communion lends itself to a non-supernatural account. The prayer of consecration (in the Book of Common Prayer) centres on the people rather than the bread and wine:

> Grant that we receiving these thy creatures of bread and wine, according to thy Son our Saviour Jesus Christ's holy institution, in remembrance of his death and passion, may be partakers of his most blessed Body and Blood.

In communion, no less than baptism, we are confirmed in our membership of Christ's body, the church. Partaking of the body of Christ does not mean 'sharing it out', like a cake cut into slices, but 'sharing in it', being a part of it. It is not the bread which is magically changed into the body of Christ: it is the worshippers sharing the bread who are confirmed as the body of Christ. That is to say, they affirm their fellowship in following the ideals focussed for them in Jesus.

I have spoken of the discipline of daily set prayers of the church and about the two great sacraments. But for many people the term 'prayer' means chiefly something personal and spontaneous, not the reading of ancient texts. This is the third element in my own spiritual diet: how is it affected by my human-centred view of religion? Solitary prayer is perhaps the form most adaptable to the new approach. A former Archbishop of Canterbury was asked by a journalist how long he spent in prayer each morning. 'One minute,' came the prompt reply; and then, after a suitable pause, 'but I spend fifty-nine minutes preparing for it.' I assume that when the journalist used the term prayer he had in mind 'talking with God', and that the archbishop took this meaning when saying that he spent only one minute doing it. This was a good answer to an impertinent question, but in more friendly company the archbishop would surely not have denied the name prayer to his whole hour. To those with ears to hear the archbishop was getting as close as one dare in his position to saying, Christian prayer is not about talking to an invisible supernatural being. It is about stillness and recollection and aligning one's will and one's actions with one's highest values.

I am reminded of another archbishop who said that religious experience is the total experience of a religious person. And of St Paul's injunction to pray without ceasing. The Christian humanist will see all of life as prayer, that is to say, as a process of bringing to bear on our world and our life those values which we call God. Teaching on prayer in recent years has been moving in this direction, and it is time for doctrine to catch up with prayer in this respect.

5

Now is Eternal Life

Writing this book I feel like the little boy in the story who called out that the emperor had no clothes on. With one significant difference: in this case 'we are the body of the emperor'. It is I and those drawn to my Christian humanism who, having called attention to the non-existence of the supernatural, have to live with our own nakedness. This is no soft option. To be without an objective God is also to be without an objective life after death, or any prospect of my individual everlasting existence. No matter how much we have fought against the parody of God as a cosmic Father Christmas, that sense of a kindly father figure behind the universe does have its comforts. And Holman Hunt's Jesus, holding his lantern and gazing benignly as 'The Light of the World', is not a bad vision as we enter upon our own final darkness. Yet all of that we are giving up, in this new, bracing, beliefless Christianity.

Teaching of this kind is unwelcome. Non-Christians, no less than the faithful, are horrified by a Christianity which is only this-worldly. Yet various surveys done in recent years show that a large number of people who call themselves Christians and attend church regularly do not believe in life after death. They would not admit it to the vicar! But they are willing to own up in the anonymity of the opinion pollster's confessional. This is one good reason for embarking on this radical pilgrimage: to let the church meet people where they are and to speak to them in their own language.

Further, in this quest to live without the consolations of everlasting life we are not alone. The Buddhist tradition has its centre in the need for us to come to terms with our fleetingness, our nothingness, our need to 'embrace the void'. Much of the Christian mystical tradition itself has centred on the need to set aside all thoughts and ideas, even of existence; to tread the way of negation and enter wholeheartedly into the cloud of unknowing. But there is also a more descriptive Christian doctrine of the afterlife, and to that we must now turn.

Biblical background

Any discussion of the Christian view of life after death has to cope with the popular notion that heaven is a nice place where good people go, and hell is a nasty place where bad people go. It is very hard to find this picture in the Bible.

In the Old Testament, the word sometimes translated 'hell' is more often called 'grave' in English. It is simply the place that everybody goes when they die. If there is any form of life there at all, it is of the most shadowy and meaningless kind, cut off alike from God and human society. The Old Testament word translated 'heaven' carries the double meaning of 'the place where God lives' and 'the sky'. It is impossible to separate the two meanings. There are other beings in heaven in addition to God, a kind of heavenly court, but no dead humans are there. They are all in the grave. Only two humans go to heaven in the Old Testament – Enoch (Gen. 5.24) and Elijah (II Kings 2.11) – and in both cases it is precisely because they *have not died but are still alive* that they go there.

In the New Testament the word translated 'heaven' carries the same double meaning as in the Old Testament. There is still no reference to any human going to heaven, except Jesus. (The phrase 'kingdom of heaven' is St Matthew's preferred form of 'kingdom of God' and refers to God's reign rather than to a place.) The word hell becomes more interesting in the New Testament. This is because, in addition to its Old Testament meaning, it is also used to translate the name of Jerusalem's municipal rubbish tip! For reasons of hygiene and lack of space, as much rubbish as possible was burned, so the site was one continuous smouldering bonfire. Hence the reference in Mark 9.48 to hell as a place where 'the fire is not quenched'.

Which brings us to the related theme of judgment. In the Old Testament, the whole idea of an afterlife comes in response to the injustice of the world, and the idea that God will set right by judgment after death all the unfairness we see here on earth. It is hardly too much to say that belief in life after death was forced upon the Jewish mind by the need for some form of ultimate judgment – both of individuals and of nations – which would set the record straight. If this world were unjust (which it clearly appeared to be) and if God were righteous (which he was sincerely believed to be) then he must have arranged an afterlife for the purpose of final judgment.

In the earliest phase of Old Testament belief, there was no life after death worth talking about. Here for example is a hymn of praise to the creator. Of all the animals, including mankind, it says:

> These wait all upon thee:
>> that thou mayest give them meat in due season.
>
> When thou givest it them they gather it:
>> and when thou openest thy hand they are filled with good.
>
> When thou hidest thy face they are troubled:
>> when thou takest away thy breath they die, and are turned again to their dust (Ps. 104.27–29).

There is no indication that the fate of humans is any different from that of all the animals. There is no idea of an immortal soul clothed in a human body. We are earthly bodies whose life ends when the breath goes out of them. Along with this picture goes the assumption that justice is both done and seen to be done on earth, e.g.

> I have been young and now am old:
>> and yet saw I never the righteous forsaken, nor his seed begging their bread (Ps. 37.25).

However, experience taught that this did not always happen, that the wicked all too often did prosper right to the end of their lives. At one stage it would have been thought fair in such a case if the wicked man's children had suffered for their father's sins. From the time of Israel's exile in Babylon, about 500 BC, such ideas became less popular. The individual began to stand out more clearly from the tribe and the family, e.g.

> What do you mean by repeating this proverb concerning the land of Israel: 'The fathers have eaten sour grapes and the children's teeth are set on edge'? As I live, says the Lord God, this proverb shall no more be used by you in Israel. Behold, all souls are mine; the soul of the father as well as the soul of the son is mine: the soul that sins shall die (Ezek. 18.2–4).

In this new climate, the only solution to the apparent injustice of God was a final judgment of the individual after death. Since the people were thought of as enlivened bodies, rather than free-floating 'souls', a general resurrection was expected as part of a last judgment.

Meanwhile two other influences were bearing upon Jewish thinking. First of all the Persian empire engulfed the Holy Land. This brought a whole new way of religious thinking, with the whole of life seen as a battle between good and evil, the forces of light and darkness. A second world was thought to exist, a parallel to this one, where rival angels fought out battles which mirrored our personal and international struggles here on earth. Then after the Persian world-view came the Greek invasion and the spread of Greek ideas including the immortality of the soul. These new ways of thinking had a deep influence on the Jewish religion and on the way it interpreted its own tradition. By the time of the early church there was a hopeless confusion of different ideas about death and judgment and heaven and hell. That confusion survives to this day.

There are several rival theories of the afterlife in the New Testament. St Luke seems to believe that judgment is immediate at the moment of death. He has Jesus tell the sympathetic thief on the cross, 'Today you will be with me in Paradise' (Luke 23.43). In the parable of the rich man and Lazarus (Luke 16.19–31), the rich man is in torment while Lazarus is comforted, and there is a gulf between them which none can cross. St John, on the other hand, speaks of a general resurrection which will be the occasion of judgment (John 5.28f.; 11.24f.). St Paul speaks of a resurrection but insists it will not be a physical resurrection (I Cor. 15.42–44). He seems to imply that only Christians will be raised, but it is not clear.

Developed Christian teaching

All the New Testament writers thought they were living in the final days before the present world order would be wrapped up once and for all. Of course they were all mistaken. Since then the church has tied itself in knots trying to put a confused mixture of theories (some not biblical at all) into one coherent account. Up to the time of the Reformation (and to this day for Catholics), the generally accepted picture was something like this:

At death the soul was separated from the body, which decayed as 'dust to dust'. The soul went to one of three places: paradise, purgatory, or hell. In paradise it would rest in peace; in purgatory it would undergo purging or cleansing before going on to paradise; in hell it would suffer punishment. You went to paradise if you had repented and died free from sin. You went to purgatory if you had repented and received forgiveness, but still had to work through the consequences of your past sins. You went to hell if you were an unrepentant sinner who refused forgiveness. (Unbaptized infants were a problem. They suffered original sin, so could not go to paradise; but they had committed no actual sin, so did not deserve purgatory or hell. A special place called limbo was invented to accommodate them!)

At the second coming of Christ there would be a general resurrection. All these souls would be re-united with their former physical bodies in order to be judged. Those from paradise, and those sufficiently cleansed from purgatory, would go to heaven and eternal bliss. Those from hell would return there to endless torment. Those still alive at the time of the second coming would be judged without dying first. Apart from Jesus himself, the only exceptions to this general picture were our old friends Enoch and Elijah, together with the virgin Mary. These three were deemed to have gone straight to heaven, body-and-soul intact, without dying and without having to wait for the general resurrection.

From Judaism the early church took over the custom of praying for the dead. It followed from the belief that physical death did not mean extinction. In time it became customary for certain pious acts, such as pilgrimages, to earn 'remission' from time in purgatory, either for yourself or your departed loved ones. You could also pay priests to say special masses for souls in purgatory. This also led to the system known as 'indulgences'.

The sixteenth-century Reformers kept the same basic picture of life after death as the mediaeval catholic church, and made one important change. Because of the abuse of the system of indulgences, they banned prayers for the dead and denied the doctrine of purgatory. Because the biblical evidence is so confused, it was quite easy for them to do this. The result is that for Protestants your fate is sealed at death, although your actual judgment may have to await the second coming and the general resurrection.

I have given this outline in some detail because 'traditional Christian teaching' on this subject is not well known! Are you surprised? In practice, I think most clergy teaching on the subject today would say something like this: First, that Christianity affirms personal existence for each of us beyond physical death. Secondly, that the quality of our life hereafter will depend in some way upon our life here, especially our response to Jesus Christ and our faith in God. Thirdly, that the guarantee of these things is the resurrection of Jesus. And finally, that as Christians we can begin to experience here and now the new quality of life which we describe as 'eternal' or 'in Christ'. As the hymn puts it:

> Now is eternal life,
>   if risen with Christ we stand. . .
> No more we fear death's ancient dread,
> In Christ arisen from the dead.

Now is eternal life

The Christian humanist who does not believe in life after death is spared the embarrassment of trying to make sense of all this confusion. But there are still issues to be faced. I am aware of three needs in particular which traditional belief in this area helps to meet: the instinct for justice, coping with grief, and a desire for meaning in life.

First, we still have to face up to the human instinct for fair play with which the Old Testament wrestled. I think it just has to be said that there is no reason why life should be fair. The world is morally neutral. Having let go the idea of an independent personal creator, we have no need to justify this. Justice after all is not a 'thing' independent of us. It is simply one of the ways in which we experience and interpret the world. It is up to us, by the way we live our lives, to bring what we call justice to a world which by its nature is impersonal. This in no way diminishes the seriousness of living 'a godly, righteous and sober life'. If anything we should be more determined to bring about justice in the world if we do not have the cosy certainty that God will take care of it all on judgment day.

Secondly, what of our wish to carry forward all the good things of this life, and especially those loving relationships which give our lives their greatest value? Are we really strong enough to give up the hope that, 'We'll meet again. . .'? I have to say that I do not know. Until I have to face the test I shall not know whether I shall cope. I wish that I could carry that hope, of course. But I cannot. Not honestly, deep down. So there is no choice in the matter. It is a deep instinct, of course. That is why so many people have believed in some kind of future life. What we have to do is to turn this instinct which pushes things out into the future, so that we can bring them back into the present. If we all accepted that we have only this life to enjoy, we might be more positive in our appreciation of it; and if we accepted that we have only a limited time to show our love and affection, we might do it with more generosity more whole-heartedly than is often the case now.

A third reason for believing in a life which extends beyond physical death is that only this can give meaning to life on earth. If three-score years and ten is the sum total of my existence, then, the argument goes, there is no purpose to my life. If death is the end of everything, then it makes a mockery of all our strivings and all our achievements. This is perhaps the most powerful reason nowadays for believing in eternal life of some kind. I said in chapter three that the deep anxiety of the world today is a sense of lostness, and a lack of purpose. Would not belief in everlasting life restore some purpose? To deny that eternity is there ahead of us looks like a counsel of despair, a too easy acceptance of the futility of human existence. This line of argument ignores the route by which we came to our present position.

Why is the Western world afflicted today by a sense of aimlessness? It is precisely because the old Christian hope, caricatured by opponents as, 'pie in the sky when you die', no longer works for people. Traditional Christianity has devalued the present world by putting all the positive emphasis on a future life. Life in this world has been characterized as short, wearisome, sinful, uncertain, frail, weak, worthless. It is a 'vale of tears' which we should be pleased to leave as soon as possible. Thus the Prayer Book burial prayer can say with no hint of irony:

Almighty God, with whom do live the spirits of them that depart hence in the Lord, and with whom the souls of the faithful, after they are delivered from the burden of the flesh, are in joy and felicity; We give thee hearty

67

thanks, for that it hath pleased thee to deliver this our *brother* out of the miseries of this sinful world. . .

This prayer, remember, was composed at a time when very few of those buried would have reached the three-score years and ten referred to earlier in the service during the reading of Psalm 90. Yet in the whole service there is no hint of sadness that a life should have been lost prematurely, no reference to any legitimate joys or creative worth of human life, and no word of comfort for the mourners. The whole theme of the service is summed up in one of its sentences: 'Man that is born of woman hath but a short time to live, and is full of misery.' The only positive note is in the plea that God might be merciful and make the future life happier than this one.

The possibility of that future life – the positive side of the message – is no longer credible, so we are left with just the negative part – the devaluing of this 'vale of tears'. Small wonder that people turn away from the church in their millions in their search for meaning. Traditional doctrine is thus the cause of the problem. It will never provide the cure. For that we need to find a way to re-affirm the value of this life, without denying the actual experience of human life both good and bad.

A clue to the answer lies in art. We do not value works of art by their size. The artist may charge more for a large canvas because it takes more time and more material, but its true value will be in the quality of the painting. The same is true of music and literature. In terms of artistic worth, a song can rival a symphony, a sonnet be the equal of a play. In a famous passage Shakespeare says that:

Now is Eternal Life

> All the world's a stage,
> And all the men and women merely players;
> They have their exits and their entrances;
> And one man in his time plays many parts. . .
>> (*As You Like It*, II.7).

This is a thought worth pursuing. A performance, like any work of art, is not judged by its length. *Hamlet* is a play in five acts. 'Shall I compare thee to a summer's day?' a sonnet of fourteen lines. They are both Shakespeare masterpieces and each has a length appropriate to its nature. If the poem were any longer it would not be a sonnet. The human life has a traditional span of seventy years. It does not need an imagined eternity to give it meaning, any more than the sonnet needs to be the length of a play, or the play needs to go on beyond three hours. In fact, in all these cases the extension would destroy the nature of the thing. Our lives will be given meaning and purpose by the way they are lived and by the quality of their performance, not by going on for ever and ever amen.

Human values

Even a sympathetic reader may feel that I have now cut off the branch I am sitting on. Having denied the existence of God, who might have provided some absolute values as a basis for this earthly life, I now make the whole possibility of a meaningful life depend upon its values. But this is the whole point of a radical Christian *humanism*. When we bade farewell to the supernatural 'other world', we did so totally. Not only the absolute existing-out-

69

there God has gone. So have the absolute existing-out-there values such as peace, joy, goodness, beauty, love, etc. The arguments we used in chapter two to show that we could have no knowledge of a supernatural God apply equally to all other supernatural beings, thoughts, ideas, concepts and words. There *is* nothing 'out there' – or if there is, we can have no knowledge of it. Those virtues I listed just now are not eternal 'things'. They are humanly created and experienced values. And none the worse for that. The only difference from the old idea that they were created by God is that we now acknowledge them to be ours: we made them, and therefore we must look after them, cherish them, and commit ourselves to them, because no one else is going to.

A common response to this interpretation of the world is great pessimism: if there are no absolute values, no absolute rights and wrongs, then surely anyone can make up their own rules and values and we shall end up in chaos. There will be no way of saying absolutely that Hitler was evil and Mother Teresa of Calcutta good. It is an open invitation to every rogue and scoundrel to make up the rules to suit himself. This reaction is understandable but misses the point: there never was any absolute way of telling good from bad. The old values were human ones even when they were believed to be eternal truths. It is human beings making human judgments who have given Hitler the thumbs down and Mother Teresa the thumbs up. And they will go on doing it as before. Sometimes there will be disagreement. Sometimes the judgment of one generation will be questioned by a later one. After all, a lot of people in the 1930s thought that Hitler *was* right. And quite a lot of things once done in the name of Christian truth are now felt to have been wrong. In general, however, there is a large area of agreement across cultures about certain moral values. This is why the idea of there being some eternal moral order, reflected in the human heart and mind, has been so persuasive in the past. None of that has changed. What has changed is that we are now able to admit that they are our decisions, our choices, and our responsibility.

A practical consequence follows from this. If we know that all our values are human, it ought to make us a little more modest in our insistence on them. When a person believes that they are the chosen instrument of God, or the champion of some other supernatural virtue, there is no limit to the claims they will make. Humanism restores some balance and sanity to outrageous pretensions. Christian humanism directs us to the Christian tradition for our choice of values in creating our own lives and giving them meaning.

6

Called upon to Proclaim

It is all very well for me to say that I have given away my old second-hand faith and discovered what I really believe, but what right do I have to do such a thing? I am not just a private individual but an authorized minister of the church. Does that not oblige me either to believe and preach the received faith or else to resign?

Authority in the church

At the time of my ordination, and every time I have subsequently taken up a new post, I have like all the clergy had to make the Declaration of Assent. This is preceded by a preface which sets out the church's own view of itself. The preface and declaration are here given in full:

Preface

The Church of England is part of the one, holy, catholic, and apostolic Church, worshipping the one true God, Father, Son, and Holy Spirit. It professes the faith uniquely revealed in the holy Scriptures and set forth in the catholic creeds, *which faith the Church is called upon to proclaim afresh in each generation*. Led by the

72

Holy Spirit, it has borne witness to Christian truth in its historical formularies, the thirty-nine Articles of Religion, the Book of Common Prayer, and the Ordering of Bishops, Priests, and Deacons. In the declaration you are about to make, will you affirm your loyalty to this inheritance of faith as your inspiration and guidance under God in *bringing the grace and truth of Christ to this generation and making him known to those in your care?*

Declaration

I do so affirm, and accordingly declare my belief in the faith which is revealed in the holy Scriptures and set forth in the catholic creeds and to which the historic formularies of the Church of England bear witness; and in public prayer and administration of the sacraments, I will use only the forms of service which are authorized or allowed by Canon.

I have italicized what seem to me to be the key clauses in this preface: *which faith the Church is called upon to proclaim afresh in each generation,* and *bringing the grace and truth of Christ to this generation and making him known to those in your care.* If the church is to take seriously the task it has set itself of proclaiming the gospel message *afresh* in each generation, then it must do just that. Trotting out the same old words time and again simply will not do. And if I am to fulfil my personal commitment to make Christ known to those under my care, then I have to present him in today's terms. I am not saying that we should water down the gospel in an attempt to make Christ acceptable. Far from it. I am saying that unless we re-present the gospel and Christ in today's language, their real message, whether of challenge or comfort, will never reach people. And by today's language I do not mean modern versions of the Bible rather than the Authorized Version. They often do more harm than good. I mean the total framework and world-view in which we live. The question then becomes, How much re-presenting and re-interpreting can we do and still claim that it is the same faith? Should we even be thinking of an unchanging core of faith?

The Preface printed above certainly does presuppose that there is such a thing as 'the faith', and gives a clear 'pecking order' when it comes to the authority of different texts relating to it. Lowest are the historic formularies of the Church of England. They are described as having *borne witness* to Christian truth. Next come the catholic creeds, in which the faith is said to be *set forth*. Finally, and carrying the greatest weight, come the holy scriptures in which the faith is *uniquely revealed*. Until recently this seemed to me a sensible and practical scheme and one which I could happily work with. Unfortunately it is based on two assumptions which I can no longer accept.

One is this idea that there is a core or essence of Christianity, in among all the less essential things. John Betjeman refers to this when he failed his divinity exams and was sent down from Oxford, because he only knew about the *inessentials*:

> . . . Still for me
> The steps to truth were made by sculptured stone,
> Stained glass and vestments, holy-water stoups,

Incense and crossings of myself – the things
That hearty middle-stumpers most despise
As 'all the inessentials of the Faith'.

As an anglo-catholic I have always sympathized with
Betjeman over this! Now as a radical I feel that he is
actually on to something very important. Partly this
concerns the practice of religion having priority over the
theory of doctrine. And partly it concerns what I now see
as a false distinction within Christian doctrine itself
between an essential core and a negotiable husk. In
presenting the faith to this generation I am bound to be
presenting a *different* faith from that which my forefathers
presented. Not just a different *interpretation* of the same
essential core, but a *different faith*. This is because there
is no essence or inner core. Re-interpretation is not like
taking the shell off a nut. It is like peeling the layers off
an onion: the interpretation goes all the way down. All is
interpretation. That *is* the essence.

The other unacceptable assumption behind the 'pecking order' is that the older a text is, the more authority it
has: the scriptures are older than the creeds which are
older than the articles. It is a general rule that any new
interpretation of the faith has to be shown to conform to
older interpretations. The idea of anything genuinely new
is effectively ruled out before the discussion starts. I can
no longer accept this as a binding principle. I do not apply
it in any other part of my life and I can see no reason to
apply it in my religion.

An example. My first degree was in chemistry. I learned
to be grateful to the early pioneers of the science – many
of them clergy of the Church of England, by the way! –

and in many cases their observations and theories were still of use. But the subject developed precisely by the older views being challenged and new ideas being put forward and tested. When a conflict of evidence arose between new and old, more work was carried out to determine which hypothesis accounted better for the observations. The most useful theory was the one adopted; and this was done in the certain knowledge that in time it would itself be superseded.

That is the way I wish to do my theology as well. It is permitted so far as the lowest level of texts is concerned. I am allowed to say, of some clause in the prayer book or the thirty-nine articles, that it is no longer helpful in dealing with an issue. I have much less leeway with the creeds. I may perhaps say that 'being of one substance with the father' is technical fourth-century language which needs putting in modern terms; I am certainly not allowed to say that even in their own terms the framers of the Nicene creed got it wrong, and that what we should be saying is that the son is not of one substance with the father! When we come to the Bible things are in some ways better and in others worse: better because the Bible is so long, and contains so many apparent internal contradictions, that no one can simply take it all at face value; but worse because there is hanging over it the belief that in some way or other it is the uniquely revealed Word of God. So it is even less permissible than with the creeds to say of any particular passage: it is plain wrong. But what makes the difference? Bible, creeds and thirty-nine articles are all human writings. In the case of the creeds we know for certain that the words were argued and fought over with great fierceness and not a little politics.

I can use and respect such texts in many ways, but I cannot agree to be bound intellectually and spiritually by their interpretations and conclusions.

Called upon to proclaim

So what am I to do? As an official minister I am required to join with the whole church in presenting the faith afresh to this generation, and to affirm my loyalty to the inheritance of faith represented by the Bible, the creeds and the articles. All of this I am eager to do. The problem is: I do not see this inheritance in the same way as those who bequeathed it to me. They thought they were passing on 'the faith', a definable object which might grow and develop but would never essentially change. Some thought it grew like a crystal, getting bigger but unchanged in shape and structure; others (more recently) thought it grew like a seed, changing radically as it grew but according to a predetermined pattern; and for others again (and for many today) it is an unchanging core of truth in a changing set of outer cultural wrappings. For me, this eternally true thing called 'the faith' is an illusion, a useful fiction to affirm our desire to stand in line with the great Christian heroes of the past. That is all right. That is my loyalty to this inheritance. The problem comes when I have to declare my belief in this fictional faith and say that I believe it to be revealed in the scriptures and set forth in the creeds. How can I? Every generation creates its own faith in and out of those texts. The faith of each century is different. Pretending that they are the same only gives ammunition to those forces within and outside the church which oppose change and innovation. The texts we have are snapshots of particular points in Christian history. I am happy to read them, learn from them, draw on them for ideas, and for support in my daily life. But I cannot be bound by them. Sometimes what they say simply does not make sense now and, as one of my teachers says, Nonsense is still nonsense, even when people talk it about God!

That is my dilemma. One way out would be to leave the church. I should then be a free agent able to believe and speak anything I chose. This is not a course I should follow from choice. There are three reasons for this.

First, there is nothing I would rather be than a priest in the Church of England. For as long as I can remember I have felt called to that office, to help others in their Christian lives. It gives me both a livelihood and also authority to exercise this ministry.

Secondly, I need the community of a church in order to explore and practise my own faith. In the history of religion, as of politics, the fate of break-away groups and individuals is not encouraging.

Thirdly, there must be many lay people who feel as I do about the Bible and creeds and need support. For me to stand aside and let the church be taken over completely by the conservatives would be to let these people down. The Church of England is historically a broad church, a church of the people, which has not demanded 'windows into men's souls'. My Christian humanism may seem rather tame compared with the dogmatic claims of the past, but it is truer to the genius of the English church than is the narrow sectarian spirit of many parishes today. Just as I need a community in which to practise my open form of religion, so lay people deserve to have parish churches where they will be given space to explore their own faith, and not have someone else's forced upon them. This will only be possible if priests with my approach are willing to stick at our posts in spite of opposition.

Having decided to stay in the church if possible, there are three options. Some clergy who find themselves in my position just keep quiet. They have gradually moved to more extreme liberal opinions and hardly dare admit to themselves that they no longer believe in the objective personal God of their youth. An obscure combination of fear and loyalty keeps them silent. Their bishop, their congregation, their family, even the God they no longer believe in, all unwittingly play their part, and the clergy may barely be aware themselves of what they are doing. It is very easy – as I know – to preach sermons which are outwardly orthodox but which thinly veil unbelief. I do not blame clergy who take this option, but it is no longer for me. I can only help the laity and fellow clergy who are in the same position if I speak out about my own faith.

A second approach is to argue that, despite appearances, my Christian humanism is the legitimate heir to the tradition *even on its own terms*. This after all was the strategy which the early church used in relation to the Jewish religion of its day. What Christianity actually did was to take the mainstays of Judaism and renounce them one by one: the temple, the food laws, circumcision, the sabbath, etc. It was to all intents and purposes a new religion. Yet by ransacking the Jewish scriptures for relevant or biddable texts, it managed to persuade itself (if not the Jews!) that it was in fact the true Israel and the rightful heir of the promises to Abraham.

A third possibility, still remaining in the church, is to

go further than this and to challenge the tradition outright to admit its mistakes. This would mean calling for radical reform in the face of radically changed circumstances, making no effort to justify this from the tradition itself.

My interim position is a combination of these last two. I wish to remain in the church and to serve its members, so I shall not be unnecessarily 'bolshie'. (It has been pointed out to me more than once that I am by nature an establishment person!) The second option is therefore my preferred one. On the other hand, there are certain fundamental errors about which I feel too strongly to keep quiet, even though they seem to be justified by the tradition. Foremost among them is precisely the way we feel ourselves bound to the past! And linked with this, we do need to get away from the idea that there is somewhere an unchanging hard core of 'the faith'. Even if I were able to justify my entire position from the Bible, I should still want to say: but I do not hold to this because it is in the Bible: I hold to it because it is true for me now!

I am conscious of the reader who has followed me so far still asking, Yes, but are you not really an unbeliever hanging on by your finger-nails to your job and your pension? Despite all you say, would it not be better either to keep quiet or to get out? The answer, inadequate as it may seem, is that I do feel called upon to proclaim the gospel in the form which I have called Christian humanism. Let me summarize the argument.

Christian humanism

There have been in the past at least two ways of talking about God. One may be called *mythological*. It entails telling a story which brings together the earthly and heavenly into a single framework: '. . . born of the Virgin Mary, suffered under Pontius Pilate, was crucified, dead and buried; he descended into hell; the third day he rose again from the dead; he ascended into heaven, and sitteth on the right hand of God the Father almighty. . .' The other may be called *parabolic*. It speaks of the earthly and heavenly as two parallel worlds in which the one mirrors all that happens in the other. It has many forms: it is the language of Daniel and Revelation in the Bible and also of Plato. In all its forms it asserts both the reality of the supernatural world and its superiority over the natural world. In the Christian tradition the parabolic has combined with the mythological language in a confusing alliance.

We must move on beyond both the mythological and parabolic ways of speaking. There is no supernatural world of real beings which either parallels or interacts with this world. Religious language does not describe things which actually exist 'out there'. If Christian doctrine were a descriptive Absolute Truth, beamed into our world from outside, then it would make no sense to go on being a Christian once you had rejected part of that teaching. But even our brief study of the history of church teaching shows that it is not Absolute Truth. Religious language is a human attempt to make sense of the human predicament. It has been fought and argued out in the rough and tumble of persecution and politics and academic dispute. This being so, to change it – and indeed to change it radically – while remaining a Christian is not only permissible but essential. A change in teaching and practice will only come if there is a clean break with the literal use of supernatural and mythological language.

But in any system based on two worlds, one superior to (yet hidden from) the other, a person in the lesser world who has access to the greater one is going to be very powerful. This gives a strong incentive to the religious establishment to support the two-world view of reality. Old Testament prophets told the people what God had in store for them. Mediaeval popes could humble great kings. Even today, astrologers can influence the decisions of presidents. Those who hold such power are not willingly going to part with it. In modern Christianity there are not many people who claim to have direct personal instant access to God's will (though some charismatics do). It is more common to study the Bible and the church's teaching from the past. But the effect is the same. These are believed to have been, in their own day, revelations, i.e. direct messages from the supernatural world. To discover God's will for us now, we must therefore study these old messages. Two things follow from this. First, there is great competition for the right to interpret this information from the past, for therein lies the power. Secondly, any new idea or action has to prove that it does not go against these old words. In this world mistakes are made and things change. But on this theory God does not change and he never makes mistakes, so all new moves must be consistent with past revelation.

We need to challenge all this for two reasons. First, so far as the church's internal life is concerned, claiming divine and supernatural authority for human rules and ideas has led to an abuse of power, and a built-in conservatism. Taking the non-existence of a supernatural

God as our working hypothesis will lead to a more open and democratic form of church life. Secondly, so far as the church's external relations are concerned, it has been marginalized because the worlds of art and science and philosophy all work from a sceptical rather than a dogmatic base. (Only conservative politics still works on the basis of a supernatural realm, and for the same reason as the church: it legitimates its power structures.) By changing its own working hypothesis, the church will be able to take up its rightful place in the creative areas of life.

Christian humanists will always be caught between traditional Christians, who denounce them because they do not accept the supernatural, and secular humanists, who ridicule them because they still practise their religion. What motive can we have for continuing the struggle? I have tried to examine my own case and have come up with the following list, in no particular order of priority:

1. It is a position which I can hold with intellectual integrity.

2. It enables me to continue in fellowship with the church and so have my own spiritual needs met.

3. My 'loyalty to the inheritance of faith', as the Declaration of Assent calls it, makes me reluctant to hand the church over to the conservatives. I believe their handling of the tradition is unhelpful and that it is not safe in their hands.

4. I feel a duty and a desire to help others who seek to keep their Christian faith alive with integrity.

5. Christian humanism offers something to those brought up within a broadly Christian culture but without any personal religion. It provides common ground on which the church and the world can meet.

6. As a provisional and non-threatening development of our tradition, it offers a positive way forward in our multi-faith and multi-cultural society.

There may be those who are sympathetic to my views, but hold back because Christian humanism lacks the element of certainty which is characteristic of all other forms of Christianity. This is the crucial point at issue. There is at the heart of the gospel a call to radical insecurity: 'Sell all that thou hast!' It is a betrayal of that call when it is turned into a cosmic insurance policy by the church: Give all that you have to us now, and we will guarantee you countless treasure hereafter! People have seen through that game. Fewer and fewer can believe it even if they want to. The need today is for a genuine response to the challenge: 'Take up thy cross and follow me.' Accept the emptiness and the futility; take up the cross; do not expect any reward; embrace the void; and you may hear that other invitation, 'Come unto me all that labour and are heavy laden. . . My yoke is easy and my burden light.' The cross and the easy yoke may be one and the same. But there is no guarantee.

We walk by faith, not by sight.

References

General

All scripture citations are from the *Revised Standard Version*, except the psalms (which are from Coverdale's translation as normally bound up with the Book of Common Prayer) and the allusions on page 84 which are deliberately quoted from memory.

Page 11
Sea of Faith Conference is an annual event run by and for the network of the same name, which also produces a quarterly magazine.
Details available from:
Ronald Pearse, 45 Middleton Place, Loughborough, Leics. LE11 2BY.

Page 17
The spacious firmament on high
Hymn by Joseph Addison (1672–1719); Hymns Ancient & Modern Revised, 170.

Page 48
Couplet from Alexander Pope (1688–1744), *Essay on Man*, cited from *The Oxford Dictionary of Quotations*.

Page 65
Now is eternal life
Hymn by G.W. Briggs (1875–1959), *Hymns of the Faith*,
1957; Reprinted by permission of Oxford University
Press.

Pages 74–75
Extract from *Summoned by Bells* by John Betjeman, John
Murray 1960, p. 96. Reprinted by permission.

For Further Reading

Armstrong, K., *A History of God*, Heinemann 1993

Barton, John, *People of the Book?*, SPCK 1988

Cupitt, Don, *Sea of Faith*, BBC 1984
____ *Radicals and the Future of the Church*, SCM Press 1989

Dawes, Hugh, *Freeing the Faith*, SPCK 1992

Goulder, Michael, & Hick, John, *Why Believe in God?*, SCM Press 1983

Houlden, J.L., *Connections*, SCM Press 1986

Hughes, Gerard W., *God of Surprises*, Darton Longman and Todd 1985

Jeff, Gordon, *Am I Still a Christian?*, Triangle (SPCK) 1992

Kuitert, H.M., *I Have My Doubts* SCM Press 1993

Wiles, Maurice, *The Remaking of Christian Doctrine*, SCM Press 1974
____ *Faith and the Mystery of God*, SCM Press 1982